The King in the Car Park

WRITTEN BY
CATRIONA CLARKE

Contents

Looking for Richard

Richard III was King of England between 1483 and 1485 and was the last English king to die in battle. It is very unusual for a king or queen not to have a grave that people can visit, but until recently no one knew exactly where Richard's grave was.

Researching Richard

Richard III has always had a very bad reputation, but some people believe this is unfair. The Richard III Society is dedicated to researching Richard and finding out exactly what sort of king he really was. Philippa Langley is President of the Scottish branch of the society.

Name: Philippa Langley

Mission: In 2009, Philippa Langley started the 'Looking for Richard' Project. She wanted to find Richard III's remains, and to give him a proper burial.

Historians knew that Richard had been buried in the **friary** of Greyfriars in Leicester, but there was no trace of the friary today. Many people believed that Richard's remains had been dug up in the 1500s and thrown into the River Soar. Langley worked with historian John Ashdown-Hill, and concluded that there was no evidence that this had happened, so the remains would still be in the friary. They strongly believed that the friary was lying underneath what was now a car park.

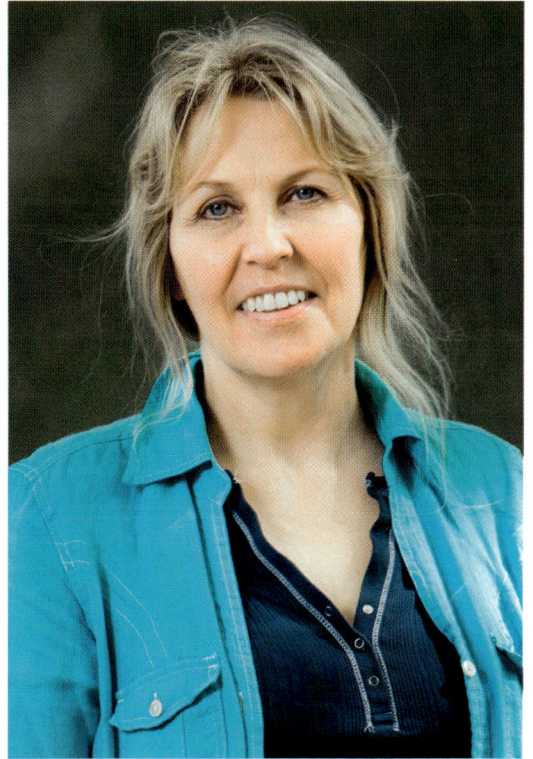

DID YOU KNOW? When Philippa Langley first visited the car park in Leicester, she had a strange feeling that she was standing exactly on top of Richard's grave. Nearby, the letter 'R' was spray-painted on the ground! She would soon find out whether she was right.

Digging Down

The Looking for Richard Project raised money to fund an **archaeological** dig in the car park. The archaeologists didn't believe they would find Richard, but they were interested in looking for the friary. The dig began on 25th August 2012.

Key players:

Richard Buckley – project manager and lead archaeologist

Jo Appleby – osteologist and archaeologist

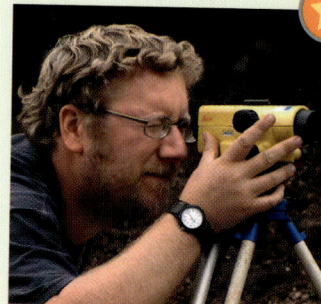

Mathew Morris – fieldwork director and archaeologist

1

On the very first day, a human left leg bone was found in the first trench. The right leg was then found next to it. The feet were missing. The team didn't know who the bones belonged to, so the remains were labelled 'Skeleton 1'.

2

The remains of the friary wall were found in the same trench.

3

When the team uncovered the rest of Skeleton 1, they saw that the grave had been dug in a hurry. It was uneven and not very deep.

DID YOU KNOW? The bones were found on exactly the same date as Richard III's burial at Greyfriars in 1485.

4

Jo Appleby uncovered the skull and saw that there was damage that could have been inflicted in battle.

5

As digging continued, the team realised that Skeleton 1 lay in the choir of a church – exactly where Richard III was said to be buried.

6

When Appleby cleared the earth around the spine, she found that the spine was shaped like the letter 'S'. Historians believed that Richard III had a curved spine, so now the team began to believe that they might have found Richard.

Could the team have found Richard III's grave on the very first day of digging? They faced a long wait to find out.

Richard or Not?

Scientists and historians spent the next few months trying to find out if Skeleton 1 was actually Richard III. There were two main strands to the investigation: the bones and Richard's relatives.

The bones

After months of studying Skeleton 1, scientists had found out that:

- the bones were from the 1400s

- they were the bones of a man in his thirties, with a diet rich in **protein**: only very rich people would have had a diet like this

- there were many injuries, including nine to the skull and facial area

- the curve in the spine showed that the person had suffered from **scoliosis.**

All of these things made it likely that it was Richard III, but final confirmation was needed.

Richard's relatives

DNA was extracted from Skeleton 1 and compared with the DNA of a man called Michael Ibsen. The historian John Ashdown-Hill had worked out that Ibsen was distantly related to Richard III's sister, Anne of York. A woman called Wendy Duldig was identified as a relative of Richard III's mother, Cecily Neville. Her DNA was tested too.

Wendy Duldig

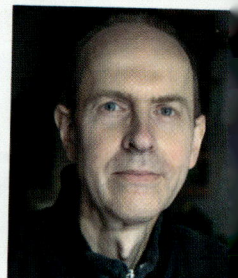

Michael Ibsen

Richard III's Family Tree

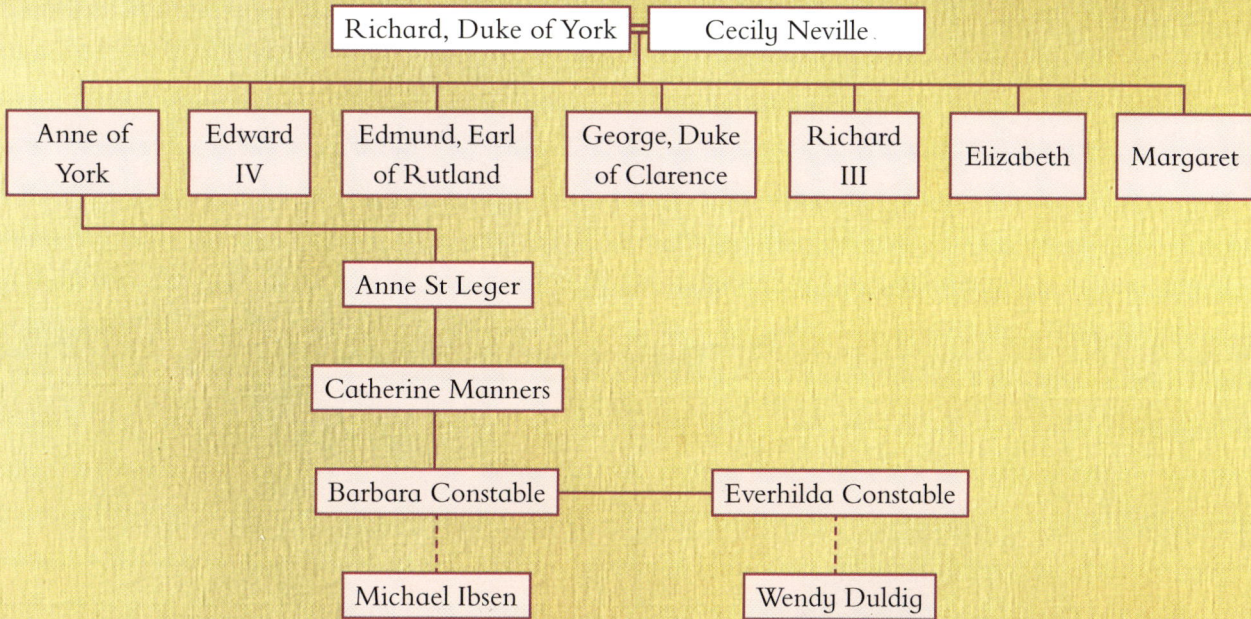

Richard, Duke of York = Cecily Neville

- Anne of York
- Edward IV
- Edmund, Earl of Rutland
- George, Duke of Clarence
- Richard III
- Elizabeth
- Margaret

Anne St Leger

Catherine Manners

Barbara Constable ——— Everhilda Constable

Michael Ibsen

Wendy Duldig

The results showed that Ibsen and Duldig both shared DNA with Skeleton 1, finally proving that the remains *did* belong to Richard III.

The face of a king

Experts used a 3D image of the skull to reconstruct what Richard might have looked like and to build a model of his face.

The world now had the chance to look at the face of a king – 500 years after he died.

England Divided

Richard was born at a time of **civil war** known as the Wars of the Roses. The royal House of Plantagenet had held the throne since 1154 and now two rival branches of the family were fighting for the throne. Long periods of peace were shattered by violent fighting.

HOUSE OF LANCASTER

LEADER:

King Henry VI
(1421 – 1471)

EMBLEM:

Red rose

HOUSE OF YORK

LEADER:

Richard, Duke of York
(Richard III's father)
(1411 – 1460)

EMBLEM:

White rose

King & Country

The king was the most powerful person in the country. Most people believed that they should be loyal to him and always obey him. The king was expected to be a good soldier, able to lead his forces into battle.

Rich landowners ruled over the people who lived and worked on their land. When they wanted to fight other landowners, the men who lived on their land did the fighting.

The people who worked on the land didn't seem powerful, but they could be an unstoppable force if they all came together to support one person.

DID YOU KNOW? Not everyone spoke English as we know it today. People spoke different **dialects** in different regions, and French was spoken in the king's court.

1452: Richard is born on 2nd October at Fotheringhay Castle in Northamptonshire. Richard's father, the Duke of York, is in conflict with the king, Henry VI.

The site where Fotheringhay Castle used to stand

1460: Richard's father and older brother Edmund die at the Battle of Wakefield.

◆

1461: Richard's brother, Edward, marches on London and becomes King Edward IV. Nine-year-old Richard is named Duke of Gloucester and is appointed Governor of the North.

◆

1471: 18-year-old Richard commands troops at the Battles of Barnet and Tewkesbury. Both battles are won and the king appoints Richard as Lieutenant of the North the following year.

1472–1474: Richard marries Anne Neville. Richard and Anne live in Middleham Castle, in North Yorkshire.

◆

1473–1476: Richard and Anne's son, Edward, is born. The exact date of birth is unknown.

◆

1482: Richard leads an army to invade Scotland. He recaptures the town of Berwick, which had been held by the Scots for 20 years. His victories in battle make him very popular.

◆

1483: Edward IV dies on 9th April.

Anne Neville, Queen of England and wife of Richard III

Taking the Crown

When Edward IV died, he left the crown to his 12-year-old son Edward. Richard was named as Lord Protector, which meant he would do most of the new king's duties until he was old enough to do them himself.

The princes in the tower

Richard moved Edward V and his nine-year-old brother (also called Richard) to the Tower of London. After 17th June 1483, the two boys were only ever seen through barred windows. Soon afterwards, Richard said that young Edward's claim to the throne was not valid, and that *he* should be King. Richard was crowned on 6th July 1483, and his nephews were never seen again.

Tower of London

What happened to the boys?

No one knows. One explanation is that Richard ordered the boys to be killed, to secure his position as King. Many people at the time saw Richard as a power-hungry villain. They thought that he planned his actions, and had wanted to be King for a long time. However, some historians today believe that Richard was reacting to events as they happened, and that he was acting for the good of the country. Either way, the rumour spread that the princes were dead and Richard's reputation was damaged forever.

DID YOU KNOW? In 1674 workmen dug up two small human skeletons at the Tower of London. People were sure that the remains belonged to the princes, and King Charles II had them buried at Westminster Abbey. We will probably never know the truth about the remains, as archaeologists are not allowed to excavate them.

Richard's Reign

Richard didn't have long to settle in as King. In Autumn 1483, the Duke of Buckingham called for people to support Henry Tudor's claim to the throne. The challenge failed, but it was a sign that things wouldn't be easy for Richard.

Profile: Henry Tudor

Born: 28th January 1457

Claim to throne: Weak

Henry's mother was a great-granddaughter of the fourth son of Edward III and his third wife.

Richard tried to capture Henry, but he escaped to France, where he was supported by the French King, Charles VIII.

In November 1484, Henry Tudor announced that Richard III was 'an unnatural tyrant' who must give up his right to rule. In May 1485, the French government gave Henry money to help him invade England.

What kind of king?

As the king, Richard had some strong points:

👑 He cared about justice and introduced important changes to the legal system to make it fairer for ordinary people.

👑 His **foreign policy** was sensible. He agreed to a truce with Scotland so that he could focus on Henry Tudor.

👑 He was brave. Men were willing to fight (and die) for him.

Richard's reign lasted only two years, so there wasn't much time for him to show what kind of king he could be.

Any good things he did were overshadowed by the way he took the throne.

Beaten at Bosworth

There is no clear account of the battle that led to Richard III's death, but we do know some things about it.

1 Henry Tudor landed in South Wales on 7th August 1485. He marched east with 5,000 men.

2 Richard called on his supporters and gathered an army of more than 10,000 men.

3 The two armies met at Market Bosworth in Leicestershire on 22nd August.

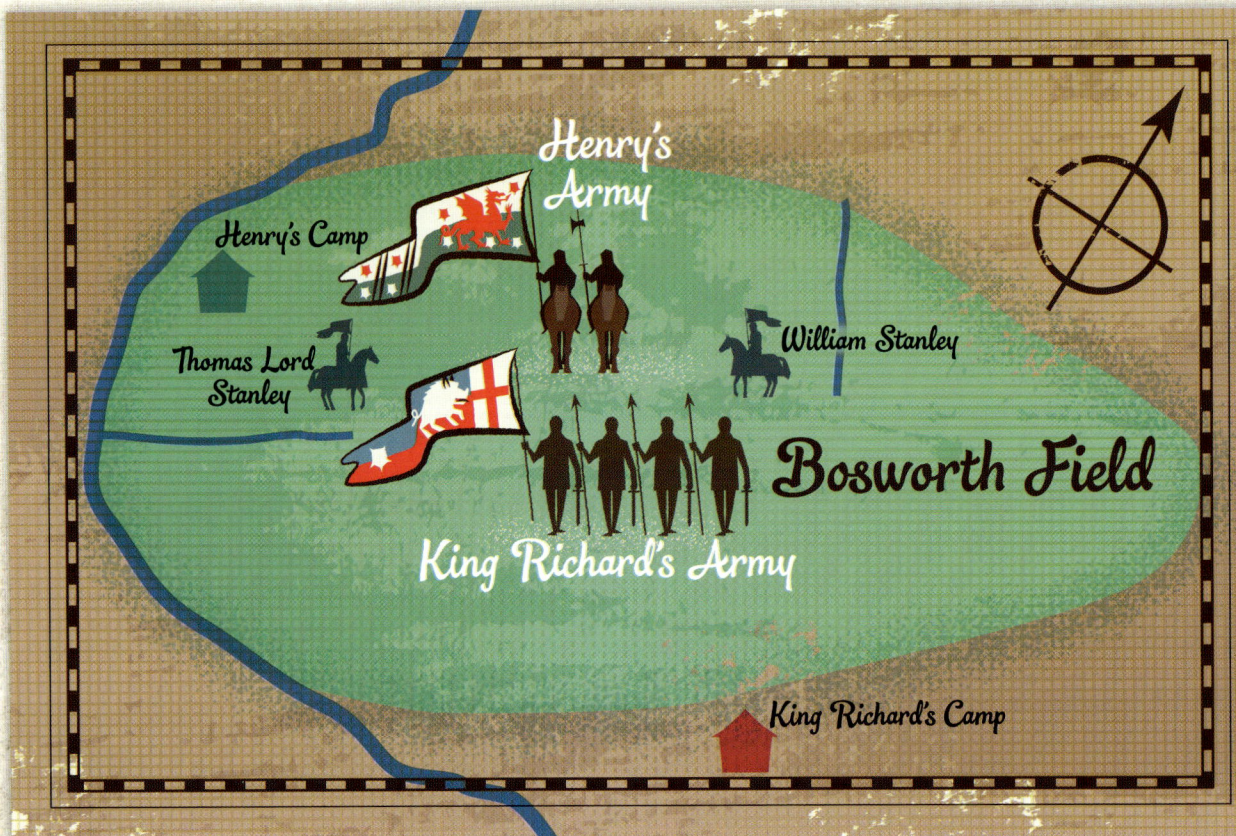

Henry's Army

Henry's Camp

Thomas Lord Stanley

William Stanley

Bosworth Field

King Richard's Army

King Richard's Camp

4 Some of Richard's supporters changed sides and fought for Henry instead.

5 Richard became cut off from the main part of his army, but continued to fight.

6 He saw Henry Tudor's flag and decided to charge, even though his supporters tried to persuade him to escape.

7 Richard was surrounded by his enemies who then attacked him.

8 Richard died on the battlefield.

Richard's body was taken to Leicester and put on public display. After two days, Richard was quickly buried in a rough hole in the choir of Greyfriars Friary. Kings are usually given grand funerals, but Henry thought Richard was a murderer who didn't deserve to be buried with honour.

DID YOU KNOW?
Richard wore a battle crown at the Battle of Bosworth. It was a specially made helmet with a crown welded to it.

Richard's Reputation

For hundreds of years after his death, Richard III was known as one of the most evil kings in British history.

Tudor times

Henry Tudor (now King Henry VII) had a very weak claim to the throne. It was important for him to show that Richard had been a bad king, so that he would look like a hero who had saved the country from Richard's rule.

Shakespeare's story

The evil version of Richard was brought to life in William Shakespeare's play *The Tragedy of King Richard III*, which was first performed around the year 1600.

In the play, Richard is shown as an ugly man with a hunched back and a withered arm. Shakespeare's Richard is evil from the beginning: plotting and murdering in order to win the throne.

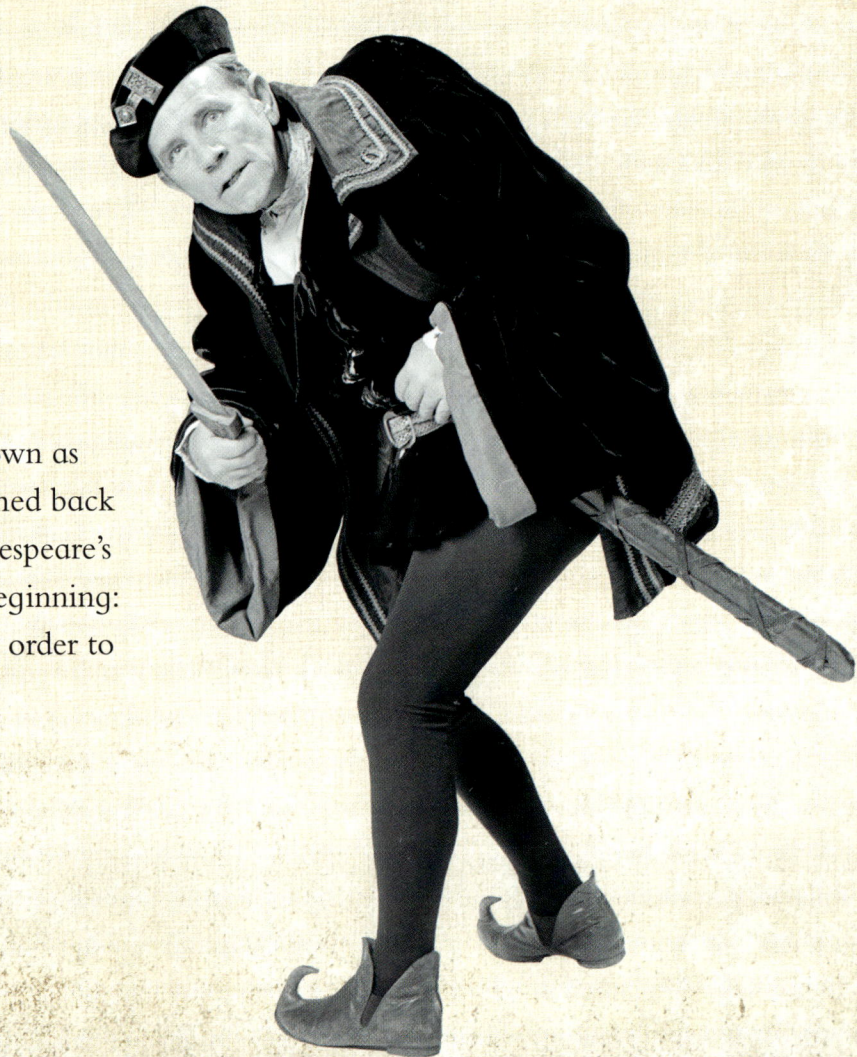

The truth?

There was some truth in this version of Richard. Although his back wasn't hunched and his arm wasn't withered, Richard did have a curved spine. We also know that people were already calling him a murderer before Henry Tudor came to power, so this idea wasn't a Tudor invention.

Richard today

The Richard III Society was founded in 1924 with a mission to clear Richard's name. The Society has worked hard to repair Richard's reputation, and today he is genuinely popular.

DID YOU KNOW? A television trial was held in 1984 to establish whether Richard III had really murdered the Princes in the Tower. He was found 'not guilty'.

Where Should Richard Rest?

Archaeologists usually bury remains as close as possible to the site where they are discovered, but some people had other ideas.

York: There was an online petition to **reinter** Richard at York Minster. Some of Richard's descendants believed this was what Richard would have wanted, because he grew up at Middleham Castle in Yorkshire. They took their case to court in 2014.

Leicester: Philippa Langley believed Richard should be **reinterred** at Leicester Cathedral. The mayor of the city was also keen for Richard's remains to stay in Leicester.

London: Some people argued that Richard should be buried at Westminster Abbey in London. Most of England's kings and queens are buried here.

The debate meant that the **reinterment** was delayed. Meanwhile, Richard's remains stayed at the University of Leicester. The question was debated in Parliament, the Queen was consulted, and Richard's descendants lost their case at the High Court. Finally, it was decided that Richard's remains should be reinterred at Leicester Cathedral.

Richard's Final Journey

On 22nd March 2015, Richard III began his final journey from the University of Leicester towards his resting place.

10.50 The coffin is brought out of a university building and there is a short ceremony. White roses are placed on the coffin by Richard's descendants and the team involved in the dig and scientific investigation.

16.50 The coffin is transferred to a horse-drawn hearse. More than 35,000 people line the streets to watch the procession.

17.45 The coffin arrives at Leicester Cathedral.

12.30 The coffin arrives at Fenn Lane Farm, very close to where Richard died at the Battle of Bosworth.

14.20 There is a short ceremony at the Bosworth Battlefield Heritage Centre.

16.30 The Mayor of Leicester welcomes the remains at the boundary of the medieval city.

The ceremony

The reinterment ceremony took place on 26th March 2015, attended by 700 people including some members of the royal family.

The ceremony was led by Justin Welby, the Archbishop of Canterbury.

The coffin was made by Michael Ibsen, one of the descendants found during the investigation. It was a simple oak coffin, with a rose and Richard's name carved into the lid.

Scientists had discovered that the actor, Benedict Cumberbatch, was very distantly related to Richard. During the ceremony, he read out a poem about Richard written by Carol Ann Duffy.

At 12.05, the coffin was lowered into the ground inside the cathedral. After more than 500 years, Richard III was finally buried like a true king.

GLOSSARY

archaeological/archaeology: scientific study of remains of past human life

civil war: war between people living in the same country

dialect: type of language spoken in a certain region or by a group of people

DNA: substance found in all plants, animals and people; everyone has unique DNA, but each person has similarities within their family

foreign policy: way in which a country's ruler or government chooses to deal with other countries

friary: building or group of buildings where monks live

osteologist: scientist who studies bones

protein: type of nutrient found in meat, fish and eggs

reinter/reinterred/reinterment: to be buried again

scoliosis: medical condition causing a sideways curve in the spine

INDEX